MORE GOOPS
AND HOW NOT TO BE THEM

*A Manual of
Manners for Impolite Infants Depicting
the Characteristics of Many Naughty and
Thoughtless Children*

with Instructive Illustrations

by GELETT BURGESS

DOVER PUBLICATIONS, INC.
New York

This Dover edition, first published in 1968, is an
unabridged and unaltered republication of the work
originally published in 1903 by Frederick A. Stokes
Company.

Standard Book Number: 486-22234-9
Library of Congress Catalog Card Number: 68-55531

Manufactured in the United States of America
Dover Publications, Inc.
180 Varick Street
New York, N. Y. 10014

CONTENTS

TABLE OF CONTENTS

INTRODUCTION

CHILDREN, although you might expect
My manners to be quite correct
(For since I fancy I can teach,
I ought to practice what I preach),
'T is true that I have often braved
My mother's wrath, and misbehaved!
And almost every single rule
I broke, before I went to school!
For that is how I learned the way
To teach you etiquette to-day.
So when you chance to take a look
At all the maxims in the book,
You 'll see that most of them are true,
I found them out, and so will you,
For if you are as GOOP derided,
You may perhaps reform, as I did!

WINDOW-SMOOCHERS

LITTLE Goops are marking
On the window pane;
I forbid, in vain!
Noses, when they're greasy,
Leave a smooch so easy!
Rub it out again!
I shall have to scold them,
For I've often told them,
Kindly, to refrain!

A LOW TRICK

THE meanest trick I ever knew
Was one I know *you* never do.
I saw a Goop once try to do it,
And there was nothing funny to it.
He pulled a chair from under me
As I was sitting down; but he
Was sent to bed, and rightly, too.
It was a *horrid* thing to do!

WHEN TO GO

When you go a-calling,
    Never stay too late;
You will wear your welcome out
    If you hesitate!
Just before they're tired of you,
    Just before they yawn,
Before they think you are a Goop,
    And wish that you were gone,
While they're laughing with you,
    While they like you so,
While they want to keep you, —
    That's the time to go!

"AIN'T"

Now "ain't" is a word
That is very absurd
   To use for an "isn't" or "aren't."
Ask Teacher about it:
She'll say, "Do without it!"
   I wish you would see if you can't!

Ain't
Isn't
Arent

NELL THE NIBBLER

SHE ate some chocolate drops at 1,
   At 2, she thought she'd take
A little jelly and a bun;
   At 3, some frosted cake.

At 4, she nibbled at a roll;
   At 5, a doughnut spied,
And ate it (all except the hole),
   And then some cookies tried.

At 6, she did n't feel quite right,
   And did n't care for dinner.
She said she had no appetite,
   With so much Goop-food in her!

JUSTICE

WHENEVER brother's sent to bed,
  Or punished, do not go
And peer at him and jeer at him,
  And say, "I told you so!"

Nor should you try to make him laugh
  When he has been so bad;
Let him confess his naughtiness
  Before you both are glad!

FRANKNESS

When you are talking, I expect
You'd better hold your head erect!
Please look me squarely in the eye
Unless you're telling me a lie.
For if you crouch and look askance,
Regarding me with sidelong glance,
I'll think it is a Goop I see
Who is *afraid* to look at me!

THE DUTY OF THE STRONG

You who are the oldest,
You who are the tallest,
Don't you think you ought to help
The youngest and the smallest?

You who are the strongest,
You who are the quickest,
Don't you think you ought to help
The weakest and the sickest?

Never mind the trouble,
Help them all you can;
Be a little woman!
Be a little man!

WALKING WITH PAPA

"Won't you walk a little farther?"
  Said a Goop to his Papa;
"It is really quite delightful,
  And we have n't travelled far;
Won't you walk a little farther,
  There's a house I'd like to see!
Won't you walk a little farther,
  Till we reach that cherry-tree?"

"Won't you carry me? I'm tired!"
  Whined a Goop to his Papa;
"And my feet are sore and weary,
  And we've gone so *very* far!
Won't you carry me? I'm tired!
  And I *can't* walk back alone!
Won't you carry me? I'm tired!"
  And the Goop began to groan.

PIANO TORTURE

Pianos are considered toys
By Goops, and naughty girls and boys;
    They pound upon the keys,
They lift the cover up, on top,
To see the little jiggers hop,
    And both the pedals squeeze!

But instruments so rich and fine
(Especially if they're not mine)
    I ought to treat with care;
So when my elder sister plays
She'll find it is in tune always,
    Nor injured anywhere!

AT TABLE

WHY is it Goops must always wish
To touch *each* apple on the dish?
Why do they never neatly fold
Their napkins until they are told?
Why do they play with food, and bite
Such awful mouthfuls?   Is it right?
Why do they tilt back in their chairs?
Because they're Goops!   So no one cares!

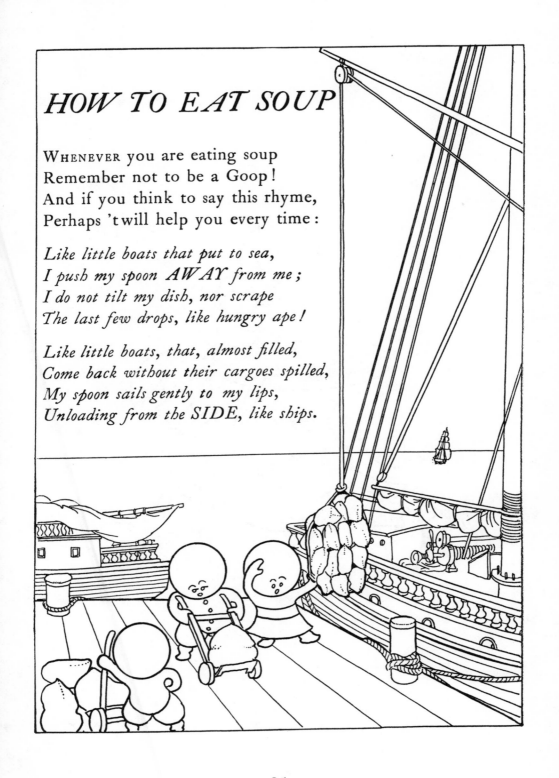

HOW TO EAT SOUP

WHENEVER you are eating soup
Remember not to be a Goop!
And if you think to say this rhyme,
Perhaps 'twill help you every time:

Like little boats that put to sea,
I push my spoon AWAY from me;
I do not tilt my dish, nor scrape
The last few drops, like hungry ape!

Like little boats, that, almost filled,
Come back without their cargoes spilled,
My spoon sails gently to my lips,
Unloading from the SIDE, like ships.

BABY'S APOLOGY

Dear little seed, queer little seed,
   Tucked into bed in the garden,
Why don't you grow?   Why, don't you know
   Baby is asking your pardon?

Out, little seed!   Sprout, little seed!
   Baby did wrong without knowing!
Hoping for you, groping for you,
   To see if you *really* were growing.

Break, little seed!   Wake, little seed!
   Baby will watch and not harm you.
Everything's bright, everything's right,
   Nothing is here to alarm you.

Dress, little seed!   Yes, little seed,
   Fold your green leaflets around you;
There, little seed!   Fair little seed,
   Baby's *so* glad he has found you!

IN THE STREET

PEELINGS on the sidewalk,
  Apple-cores and all,
Kick them in the gutter;
  Save some one a fall!
Barrel hoops, glass, and cans,
  And wires in the street,
Kick them in the gutter;
  You'll save some horse's feet!

SICK FURNITURE

Sitting on the table,
Standing on the chairs,
That's the way the legs are broken
and the cushion tears!
How'd you like to pay the bill for varnish and repairs?

BORROWED PLUMES

Don't try on the wraps,
The bonnets and caps
   Of company coming to call!
Admire, if you please,
But garments like these
   Should always feel safe in the hall!

THE GOOP PICNIC

THEY came to the best sort of place for a rest,
   On the grass, with the trees overhead,
They sat down in a bunch and they opened their
      lunch,
   And they had a be-autiful spread!

And when they were done, and they'd had all their
      fun,
   They proved they were Goops, or were blind;
For they picked up their wraps and they left all their
      scraps
   For the *next* picnic party to find!

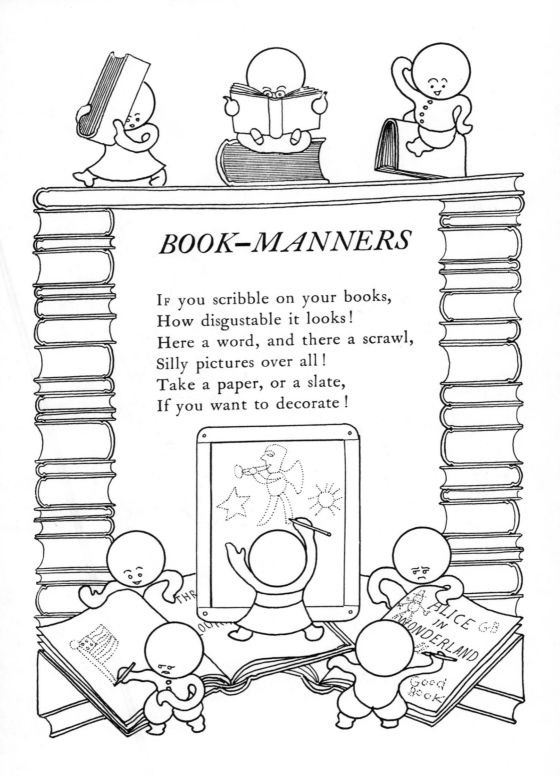

BOOK—MANNERS

IF you scribble on your books,
How disgustable it looks!
Here a word, and there a scrawl,
Silly pictures over all!
Take a paper, or a slate,
If you want to decorate!

POOR MOTHER!

Oн! Isn't it shocking!
Just look at your stocking!
 Just look at your brand new boots!
Your waist is all torn
And your trousers are worn —
 Just *look* at the holes in your suits!

Your father is working
All day, without shirking,
 To pay for the clothes that you wear;
Your mother is mending
All day, and attending
 To you, with the kindest of care.

And so, while you 're playing,
Think of father, who 's paying,
 And mother, who 's working so hard;
While you kneel on your knees,
Or climb up the trees,
 Or make your mud pies in the yard!

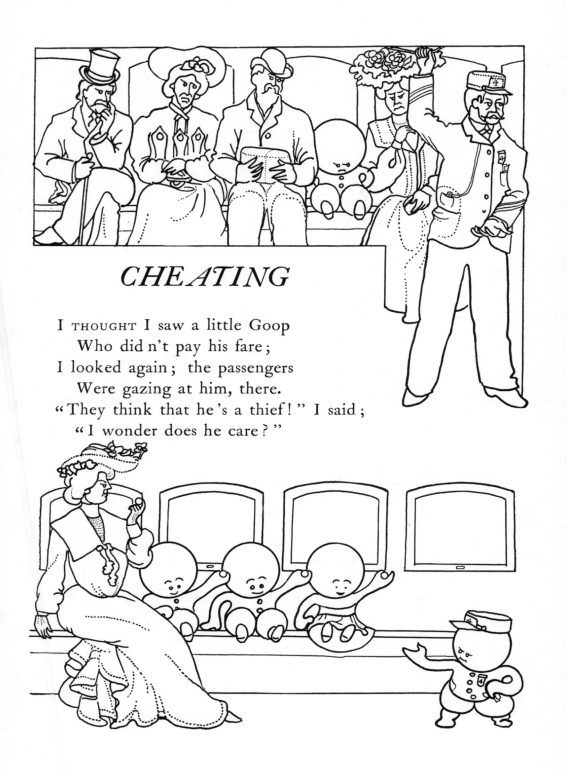

CHEATING

I THOUGHT I saw a little Goop
   Who did n't pay his fare;
I looked again; the passengers
   Were gazing at him, there.
"They think that he's a thief!" I said;
   "I wonder does he care?"

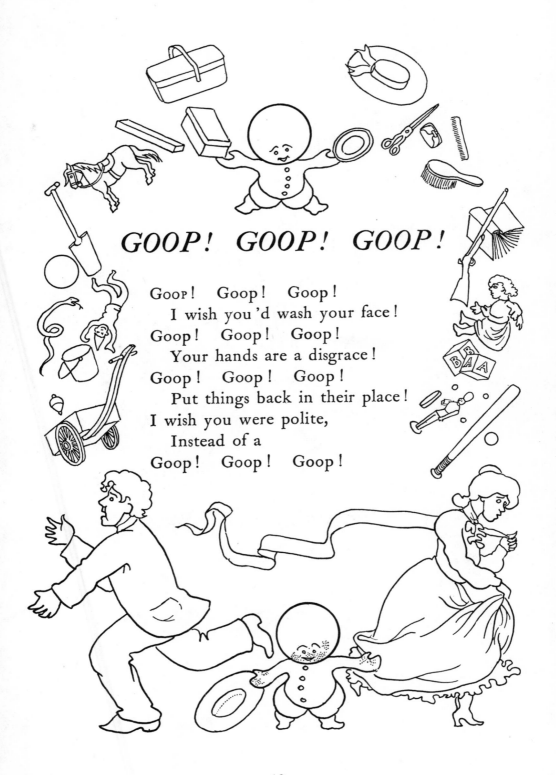

GOOP! GOOP! GOOP!

Goop!   Goop!   Goop!
    I wish you'd wash your face!
Goop!   Goop!   Goop!
    Your hands are a disgrace!
Goop!   Goop!   Goop!
    Put things back in their place!
I wish you were polite,
    Instead of a
Goop!   Goop!   Goop!

VISITING

When a Goop goes out to visit,
'Tisn't very pleasant, is it,
    To hear him ask his friends for
        things to eat?
And to hear the little sinner
Say he wants to stay to dinner
    Is a piece of impoliteness hard to
        beat!
"*Mother said that I could stay*
"*If you asked me!*" is the way
    That a Goop will make them ask
        him to remain.
It is better to be slighted
Than to stay when not invited,
    For they *never* ask a Goop to
        come again!

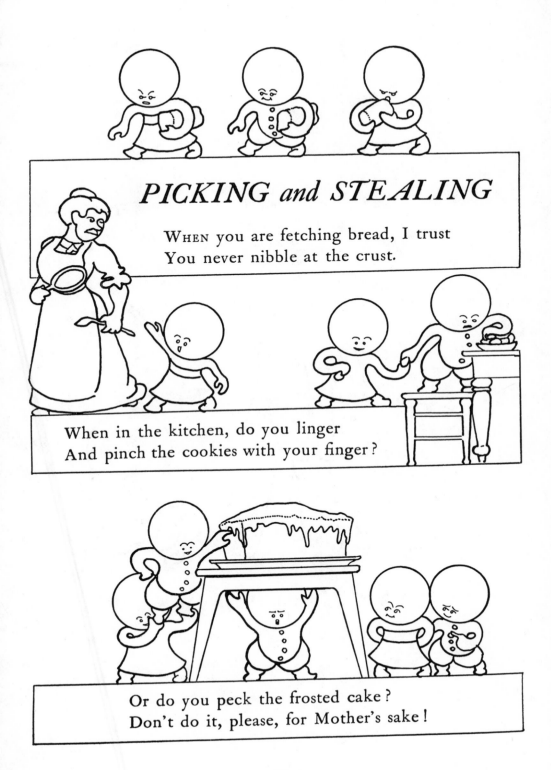

PICKING and STEALING

WHEN you are fetching bread, I trust
You never nibble at the crust.

When in the kitchen, do you linger
And pinch the cookies with your finger?

Or do you peck the frosted cake?
Don't do it, please, for Mother's sake!

LOYALTY

MOTHER's found your mischief out!
  What are you going to do?
Cry and sulk, or kick and shout?
Tell your mother all about
  Brother's mischief, too?

Or,
Take your punishment, and say,
  " I 'll be better, now!"
Never mind the horrid way
Brother treated you, at play;
  Don't tell it, anyhow!

It is the Goops,
  who have no shame,

    Who say,

    "'Twas some one else to blame!"

INDOLENCE

THERE was a Goop who lay in bed
Till half-past eight, the sleepy-head!
He could n't find his stockings, for
He 'd thrown them somewhere on the floor!
He could n't find his reading-book;
He had forgotten where to look!
His breakfast grew so very cold,
This lazy Goop began to scold;
And then he blamed his mother, kind!
"You made me late to school!"
                          he whined.

THE LAW OF HOSPITALITY

THERE is a very simple rule
    That every one should know;
You may not hear of it in school,
    But everywhere you go,
In every land where people dwell,
    And men are good and true,
You'll find they understand it well,
    And so I'll tell it you:

To every one who gives me food,
    Or shares his home with me,
I owe a debt of gratitude,
    And I must loyal be.
I may not laugh at him, or say
    Of him a word unkind;
His friendliness I must repay,
    And to his faults be blind!

THE FLOWER HOSPITAL

I DREAMED I found a sunlit room
Filled with a delicate perfume,
Where, moaning their sweet lives away,
A thousand lovely flowers lay.
They drooped, so pale, and wan, and weak,
With hardly strength enough to speak,
With stems so crushed and leaves so torn
It was too dreadful to be borne!
And one white lily raised her head
From off her snowy flower bed,
And sighed, " *Please tell the children, oh !*
They should not treat the flowers so !
They plucked us when we were so gay,
And then they threw us all away
To wither in the sun all day !
We all must fade, but we'll forgive
If they'll let other flowers live !"

PUPPY GOOPS

CANDY in the cushions
  Of the easy-chair;
Raisins in the sofa —
  How did they get there?
The little Goop who's greedy
  Does it every day,
Like a little puppy,
  Hiding bones away!

EXAGGERATION

Don't try to tell a story
　　To beat the one you 've heard;
For if you try, you 're apt to lie,
　　And *that* would be absurd!

Don't try to be more funny
　　Than any one in school;
For if you 're not, they 'll laugh a lot,
　　And think you are a fool!

NOISE! NOISE! NOISE!

Do you slam the door?
  Do you drag your feet?
Making noise enough for four
Hundred thousand Goops, or more,
  Tearing up the street?

Clattering down the stairs,
  Storming through the hall,
Pounding floors, upsetting chairs,
Do you think your father cares
  For your noise, at all?

STEALING RIDES

I THOUGHT I saw a little Goop
  Who hung behind a cart;
I looked again.   He'd fallen off!
  It gave me *such* a start!
"If he were killed, some day," I said,
  "'T would break his mother's heart!"

UNTIDY GOOPS

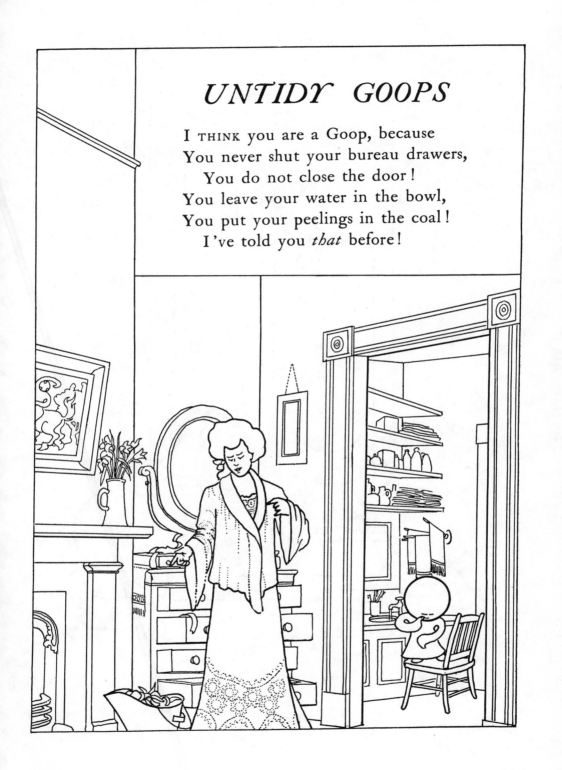

I think you are a Goop, because
You never shut your bureau drawers,
　　You do not close the door!
You leave your water in the bowl,
You put your peelings in the coal!
　　I've told you *that* before!

A GOOP PARTY

"Please come to my party!" said Jenny to Prue;
"I'm going to have Willy, and Nelly, and you;
I'm going to have candy and cake and ice-cream,
We'll play *Hunt-the-Slipper*, we'll laugh and we'll scream.
We'll dress up in caps, we'll have stories and tricks,
And you won't have to go till a quarter past six!"
But alas! When she mentioned her party, at tea,
Her mother said, "No! It can't possibly be!"
So Jane had to go and explain to her friends,
And that is how many a Goop party ends!
Just speak to your mother *before* you invite,
And then it's more likely to happen all right!

INQUISITIVENESS

I GAVE a letter to a Goop
To take to Mrs. Bird;
And what d' you think he went and did?
He read it, every word!
Now, isn't that the rudest thing
That you have ever heard?

Why, he would peep through keyholes,
And listen at the door!
And open parcels, just to see
What came from every store!

Now, have you ever *ever* heard
Of such a Goop before?

DON'T BE GOOD

Just because you want to go
To the circus, or the show;
But, when all your fun is o'er,
Be as good as you were before!

DON'T BE BAD

Just as long as you dare to be,
Because your mother does n't see.
Do not wait for her to scold,
But be just as good as gold!

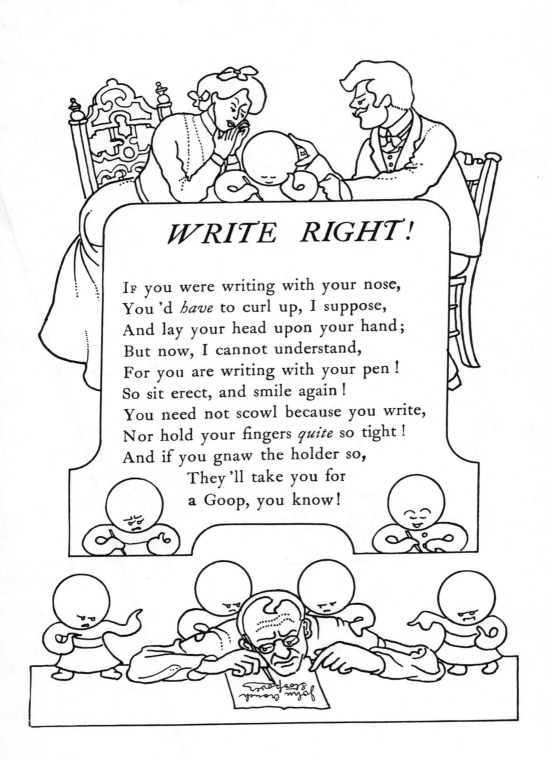

WRITE RIGHT!

IF you were writing with your nose,
You'd *have* to curl up, I suppose,
And lay your head upon your hand;
But now, I cannot understand,
For you are writing with your pen!
So sit erect, and smile again!
You need not scowl because you write,
Nor hold your fingers *quite* so tight!
And if you gnaw the holder so,
They'll take you for
a Goop, you know!

WET FEET

Down the street together,
In the rainy weather,
  Went a pair of little boys
    along;
One of them went straying
In the gutters playing,
  Doing all his mother said was
    wrong;

One of them went dashing
Into puddles splashing,
  Under dripping eaves that
    soaked him through;
One of them avoided
All the other boy did,
  Dodging all the slimy, slushy
    goo.

One of them grew chilly;
Said he felt so ill he
  Knew he'd caught a cold,
    and coughed a lot!
The other was so warm he
Said he *liked* it stormy!
  Which of them was Goop,
    and which was not?

DRESS QUICKLY!

ALL your life you'll have to dress,
Every single day (unless
You should happen to be sick),
Why not learn to do it quick?
Hang your clothes the proper way,
So you'll find them fresh next day;
Treat them with a little care,
Fold them neatly on a chair;
So, without a bit of worry,
You can dress in quite a hurry.
Think of the slovenly Goops, before
You strew your clothing on the floor!

INK, ink!   What do you think!
You're sure to be stained, if you play with the ink!
You're sure to get black, if you play with the ink-well,
Before you begin it, just stop once, and think well!
All over your fingers, all over your face,
All over your clothes, and all over the place!
Your mother'll be angry, your father'll say, "*There!*
I said not to touch it; you said you'd take care!"

When Goops are so mischievous, they have to drink
Forty-four dozen bottles of raven black ink!

THE REASON WHY

Everybody liked Ezekiel.
  Why?
You could scarcely find his equal.
  Why?
If he made a mistake,
  He said he was wrong;
If he went on an errand,
  He wasn't gone long;
He never would bully,
  Although he was strong!

Everybody hated Mello.
  Why?
He was such a surly fellow.
  Why?
If you asked him for candy,
  He'd hide his away;
He never would play
  What the rest wished to play;
He would say *horrid* words
  That he ought n't to say!

IN GOOP ATTIRE

I'LL make you a dress of a towel,
  And trim it all over with soap,
With a sponge for a hat
And a wet one, at that!
  And *then* you 'll be happy, I hope!
You may act like a Goop, if you please,
In garments constructed like these!

But now, while you 're dressed up so neatly,
  Don't wipe off your hands on your frock!
The smooching that lingers
When you wipe off your fingers,
  Will give your dear mother a shock!
The result will be even more shocking,
If you wipe off your shoes on your stocking!

IMPOSSIBLE!

THERE once was a Goop (*it is hard to believe*
Such unpleasant behavior of you!)
Who always was wiping his nose on his sleeve;
I hope that this Goop was n't you!
He always was spitting (for fun, I suppose),
I couldn't believe it of you!
And putting his fingers up into his nose;
I KNOW that this Goop was n't you!

A PUZZLE

THERE are about a thousand things
    I'm not allowed to do;
Most everything I'm fondest of
    I'm told is wrong—are you?

They say, "*Please don't do that, my child!*"
    They say, "*You mustn't, dear!*"
I hope sometime I'll learn what's right,
    For now it seems so queer!